Apsley House
The Wellington Collection

Julius Bryant

Introduction

Standing at Hyde Park Corner on central London's busiest thoroughfare, Apsley House is one of the most conspicuous residences in London. Yet, of the thousands that pass it daily, few realise its historic significance, or appreciate the splendours that lie within. From the sober neoclassical façades, Apsley House could be mistaken for an embassy or a grand club. But within lies a collection of nearly 3,000 fine paintings, sculptures, works of art fashioned in silver, porcelain and porphyry, swords, batons and orders – the gifts of emperors, tsars and kings to Britain's greatest military hero.

As the former home of the 1st Duke of Wellington (1769–1852), Apsley House has been a national shrine to the victor of Waterloo, the liberator of Europe from Napoleon, almost from the day he bought it in 1817, two years after the battle. The house is the result of two distinct phases of construction. Robert Adam built the original house between 1771 and 1778 for Henry Bathurst, 1st Baron Apsley. In 1807 he sold the house to Marquess Wellesley, older brother of Wellington. In 1817, Wellington bought the lease and employed Benjamin Dean Wyatt over the following years to enlarge and remodel the property. Although Wyatt's alterations were extensive, parts of Adam's design and decoration are still visible.

Over the next 35 years, the duke filled his London home with trophies, paintings and portraits illustrating his achievements. Many of Wellington's own visitors felt his house looked more like a museum than a home. As one of London's few surviving aristocratic town houses, however, Apsley House also reveals a way of life now lost from the capital. Most great families eventually sold up and withdrew to the country with their finest treasures, but the Dukes of Wellington kept their London house, and the family still lives in the house today.

Above: Trompe l'oeil cameo portrait of the 1st Duke of Wellington by William Grimaldi (1751–1830) (Ashmolean Museum)

Facing page: View of the principal staircase with the colossal marble statue by Antonio Canova of Napoleon, Wellington's greatest military opponent

The Tour

Apsley House is much more than a splendidly restored historic house, a great collection, a national memorial and a major art gallery. It is a celebration of the Regency taste in art, design and interior decoration. The treasures associated with Wellington and Napoleon evoke an age when the balance of power in Europe was shared between absolutist and constitutional monarchs, seeking to keep the peace through their ministers and generals, while fearing revolution at home. Apsley House conveys the character and values of London's fashionable society in this imperial era, when Britain enjoyed its greatest influence in Europe, thanks to the success of its most celebrated military commander.

FOLLOWING THE TOUR

The tour of the house starts in the entrance hall and follows a suggested route through all parts of the property open to the public. The numbers beside the headings highlight key points on the tour and correspond to the small numbered plans in the margins.

THE HOUSE

Apsley House is the product of two very different styles of building and decoration. It was originally built between 1771 and 1778 for Henry Bathurst, 1st Baron Apsley, after whom the house is still named. He employed the fashionable architect Robert Adam and the project was one of only three large central London houses both designed and furnished by Adam. The neat, brick-built town house was completed in 1778 at a cost of £10,000. It was decorated in the neoclassical style for which Adam was famed. Although later alterations have obscured or destroyed much of Adam's work, elements of his original designs are still in place today.

In 1807 Apsley House was purchased by Marquess Wellesley, who had just returned from India where he had been Governor General. In 1817 the lease was purchased by Arthur Wellesley, the 1st Duke of Wellington. Following the duke's victories over Napoleon's forces, he had been granted £700,000 by the grateful nation. This was intended to help construct a 'Waterloo Palace' for him and his heirs in the country. The duke later expanded Apsley House, employing the architect Benjamin Dean Wyatt (1775–1855) to enlarge and remodel the property. Wyatt's alterations were on a grand scale, and included re-facing the entire house in Bath stone and adding a massive two-storey extension.

The house as it appears today is largely a product of the 1st Duke's refurbishments. In 1947 Gerald Wellesley, 7th Duke of Wellington, generously gave the house and collections to the nation.

▣ THE ENTRANCE HALL

Stepping from the bustle of Hyde Park Corner into the sudden calm of the hall today, visitors enjoy a contrast that would have been appreciated in the same way by the 1st Duke of Wellington's guests and admirers. The roaring haste of the traffic is muffled and then silenced by the closing door. This entrance hall was created as part of the remodelling carried out by the 1st Duke and his architect, Benjamin Dean Wyatt, between 1828 and 1830. Adam's original front door had opened into what is now the inner hall.

In Wellington's own day, visitors entered under the suspicious gaze of a footman, whose

A WELLINGTON BOOT
Or the Head of the Armye

draught-proof porter's chair can still be seen. Those who came as Wellington's admirers, with no claim on his time, might be shown no further than the 'Museum', the room off the entrance hall, which still contains displays of the duke's memorabilia and victory gifts. Acquaintances of the duke might hope to be directed to the chairs in the inner hall to wait. Business callers, however, might remain in the entrance hall making use of the six chairs, the table 'with oilcloth cover' and the 'bronze umbrella stand', protected against the draught of the opening door by the 'high six-fold screen covered with scarlet cloth and mouldings', described in an inventory of 1854.

No paintings or sculptures are recorded here in the 1st Duke's day but by 1857 his son had installed busts of King George III, Prince Albert and the 1st Duke of Wellington; by 1882, Classical busts of Cicero, Athena and Septimius Severus, together with a modern bust of Alexander the Great and a statue of Eros, had been added. Wellington's functional entrance hall had become the first room of a sculpture gallery that leads into the 1st Duke's display in the inner hall.

Above, left: 1827 caricature of Wellington as a Wellington Boot by Paul Pry (William Heath, 1795–1840)

Facing page: A detail of the silver-gilt Portuguese Service on display in the State Dining Room, with the Waterloo Gallery glimpsed beyond

CUTAWAY VIEW
OF APSLEY HOUSE

1 Entrance hall

2 Inner hall

3 Principal staircase

4 Piccadilly Drawing Room

5 Portico Drawing Room

6 Waterloo Gallery

7 Yellow Drawing Room

8 Striped Drawing Room

9 Octagon Passage

10 State Dining Room

11 Slip Passage

12 Museum

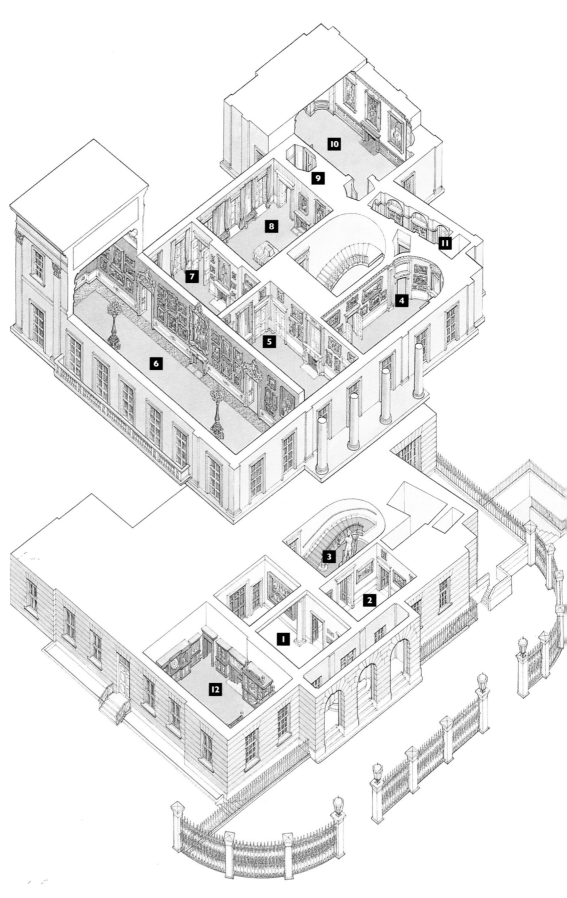

❷ THE INNER HALL

This was the original entrance hall of the house, which Adam called the 'Anti-room'. A survey of 1828 describes it as 'paved with Portland Stone … with a Valet's Room and closet on the east side'. Stairs to the basement now fill the site of the closet but the 'Valet's Room' continues in use as the manager's office. The bronze statue on its carved granite pedestal represents the Prussian Field Marshal, Prince von Blücher, and was placed here by Wellington as a memorial to his friend and ally against Napoleon. It is a copy by Christian Daniel Rauch (1777–1857) of a monument by the same artist, formerly at Breslau, that Wellington saw unveiled in 1826. The duke also displayed an impressive collection of marble busts in this room. The three French mahogany Empire-style side tables with granite slab tops, made in about 1810 (on loan from the Duke of Wellington's family) were also here. The present Minton mosaic tile floor and cast-iron radiator covers were probably installed in about 1860. The mahogany doors date from 1828–30 when Wyatt converted Adam's entrance hall. The paintwork, imitating marble and stone blocks, is a re-creation from 1995.

Top: The inner hall in about 1900, filled with sculpture
Left: A bronze statue of Prince von Blücher, Wellington's ally against Napoleon, by Christian Daniel Rauch (1777–1857). It stands on a granite base on loan from the Duke of Wellington's family

▣ PRINCIPAL STAIRCASE

Entering the stairwell visitors encounter one of the most extraordinary works of art in Britain, the colossal marble statue *Napoleon as Mars the Peacemaker* by the Italian sculptor, Antonio Canova (1757–1822). Today the sculpture may prompt smiles because of its nudity, but to the sculptor, then the leading artist in Europe, this was a work of great integrity.

Commissioned by Napoleon during his period as First Consul, Canova sought to emulate the example of antique emperors, who were shown as gods in ideal nude form. Canova's sculpture was carved from a single block, with the exception of the left arm, and was finished in Rome in 1806. But it did not arrive in Paris until 1811, by which time Napoleon was Emperor. By then in his early forties, he preferred a more modest self-image. Declaring it to be '*trop athletique*', Napoleon insisted Canova's masterpiece remain covered up in the Louvre. After Waterloo, Canova endeavoured to buy the sculpture back but in 1816 the British Government bought it for 66,000 francs and the Prince Regent (later King George IV) presented it to the Duke of Wellington. Wellington could hardly refuse such a gift. He admired Napoleon and acquired several portraits of him. The stairwell was the only possible location for the sculpture at Apsley House. Even so, the floor underneath the statue had to be reinforced with a brick pillar to support its great weight. Robert Adam's plans of 1771 reveal that the stairs originally rose from the ground to first-floor level behind columned screens and went no further. The present recasting of the room dates from Wyatt's modifications in 1829, by which stage the Canova sculpture was already in place. The ceiling plasterwork also dates from this time and includes a 'W' beneath a ducal coronet; as it does not appear in Wyatt's original design, this detail must have been his client's contribution.

Behind the closed doors facing the statue a secondary staircase links the basement to the upper floors of this five-storey house. The other pair of doors leads to the 1st Duke's library. Today both sets of doors lead to the private apartments of the present Duke of Wellington and his family.

Right: The stairwell, showing the plasterwork ceiling decorated with a 'W' beneath a ducal coronet

Left: Napoleon as Mars the Peacemaker by Antonio Canova (1757–1822), 1802–6

◼ THE PICCADILLY DRAWING ROOM

This room was one of Adam's finest interiors for the house, and his chimneypiece, ceiling and frieze still survive. The room now presents the taste of the 1st Duke of Wellington and Benjamin Dean Wyatt, following their modification and redecoration of the house between 1828 and 1830. A plan by Robert Adam shows this room with an alcove entrance, a screen of two columns across the curved end and niches flanking the fireplace. Wyatt replaced the niche to the left of the fireplace with a doorway when the new dining room was built in 1820, to provide access between these two rooms. The niche to the right of the fireplace was probably removed at the same time.

The Italian composer of operas, Giacchino Rossini, performed at Apsley House on 24 June 1824, accompanied by the star opera singer Madame Pasta. Their recital was probably given in this room, and Rossini may have performed on the zebrawood octagon piano, made by Pape of Paris and London, which survives in the Duke of Wellington's family collection. An inventory of 1854 records the furniture in the Piccadilly Drawing Room, including a central square ottoman (a four-sided sofa), another ottoman fitted to one corner of the room, two bookcases in rosewood and Boulle (brass and tortoiseshell) and two card-tables, also in rosewood and Boulle. The present restoration of Wyatt's decorative scheme dates from 1980, when the walls were hung to recreate the yellow striped 'tabaret' (a silk satin fabric) as described in the 1854 inventory. On the wall opposite the windows hangs the painting by David Wilkie, *Chelsea Pensioners Reading the Waterloo Despatch*. Outside Chelsea Hospital on 22 June 1815, a Chelsea Pensioner reads aloud the *Gazette of Waterloo*, the official account of victory over Napoleon. Among some 50 figures there are more than 15 character studies, including a black dog known as 'the Old Duke', which followed the Blues regiment through Spain.

Wellington commissioned this painting in 1816, the year after Waterloo, as 'a parcel of old soldiers … at some public-house in the King's Road, Chelsea'. He must have intended it as a tribute to his troops, in the manner of the anecdotal Dutch genre paintings he was buying in Paris at that time, many of which still hang in this room today. This was Wellington's most expensive painting: he paid Wilkie £1,260 for it. When it was exhibited at the Royal Academy in 1822, hung next to Thomas Lawrence's portrait of the duke, a rail had to be installed to keep the jostling crowds at bay. In 1841, Wellington bought (for £525) *The Greenwich Pensioners Commemorating Trafalgar*, which had been painted between 1818 and 1835 by John Burnet, on speculation. This painting also hangs in this room.

Above: Chelsea Pensioners Reading the Waterloo Despatch, 1816–22, by David Wilkie (1785–1841)

Facing page: View of the Piccadilly Drawing Room

Below: Achilles by Richard
Westmacott, unveiled in
honour of Wellington by the
women of Britain in 1822
Right: Achilles in the Sulks by
Thomas Howell Jones, 1827,
showing Wellington after he
had resigned as Commander-
in-Chief, with the Achilles
statue outside the window
(Leeds Museums & Galleries)

Above: Hyde Park Corner
photographed from the air in
the 1930s, showing Apsley
House at the end of a row
of houses along Piccadilly
Right: The Wellington Arch in
about 1860, with the giant
bronze figure of the Duke
designed by Matthew Cotes
Wyatt (brother of Benjamin
Dean Wyatt, Wellington's
architect for Apsley House)

THE SETTING

From the windows of the Piccadilly Drawing,
Room, visitors can appreciate the setting of Apsle
House, standing on Piccadilly, at the formal
entrance to Hyde Park. To the south and east lie
Buckingham Palace, its walled gardens, and Green
Park. When Apsley House was first built, this
fashionable Mayfair location was right on the
western edge of London, with fine views of the
surrounding parks. Although there was a great
deal of building nearby from the 18th century
onwards, it was not until 1961–2 that Apsley
House was isolated in its current position, when
Park Lane was diverted to Hyde Park Corner
and the houses immediately to the east of
Apsley House were demolished, cutting it off
from Piccadilly.

The house nonetheless retains some of the
grandeur of its setting, in the various monuments
and sculptures that surround it. The Piccadilly
Drawing Room gives a good view of the
Wellington Arch, which can also be visited.
Erected between 1828 and 1830 by the architect
Decimus Burton (1800–81), it originally stood in
line with the present Hyde Park Screen
(immediately to the west of Apsley House),
created at the same time by the same architect,
to form a grand entrance to Buckingham Palace
gardens and Green Park from Piccadilly. Burton
intended it to be decorated with sculpture
celebrating the defeat of Napoleon, but the
project ran over-budget and only some of the
carvings were in place by the time work finished
in 1830. By 1838, plans were underway to place
on top of the arch a statue in honour of the
Duke of Wellington. The final design, a giant
bronze equestrian statue of the duke, was
installed, despite controversy, in 1846. Rows over
the statue continued unabated, and in 1883, wher
the arch was moved to its present position to
ease traffic congestion at Hyde Park Corner, the
statue was dismantled. It was moved to the
military training school at Aldershot, where it
remains. In 1888, another statue of Wellington wa
unveiled opposite Apsley House to replace the
giant equestrian statue. This was designed by Sir
Joseph Edgar Boehm (1834–90).

While the Wellington Arch was being designed
and built, another arch to commemorate Britain's
victories in the Napoleonic Wars was being

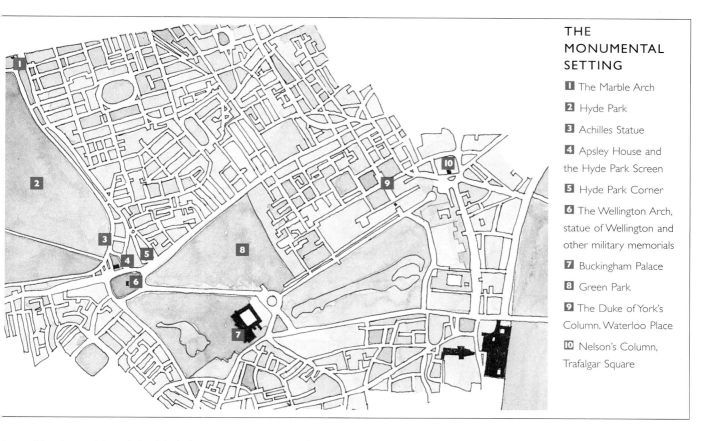

lanned by the architect John Nash. It was to tand outside Buckingham Palace, which Nash was working on at the time. Due to disputes and nancial difficulties, the completed Marble Arch was much more modest than the original designs.

was moved to its present location in 1850–1, to llow for an extension to Buckingham Palace.

A more personal tribute can be glimpsed from he window of the State Dining Room in winter, when the trees have lost their leaves. The bronze tatue of Achilles by Richard Westmacott 1775–1856), standing in Hyde Park, was raised in onour of the Duke of Wellington in July 1822. unded entirely by British women, the naked gure, cast from captured cannon, was soon icknamed 'the Ladies' Fancy Man'. Britain's first utdoor nude statue, it caused considerable ebate. Predating the Marble Arch and the Vellington Arch, it was the first of several nonuments erected nearby to honour individual articipants in the wars against the French. rederick Augustus, Duke of York and Commander-in-Chief of the army from 1798 to 809 and 1811 to 1827, had a statue erected to m in 1834. Wellington chaired the public

meeting to inaugurate the fund for the memorial. The statue was designed, like *Achilles*, by Richard Westmacott; it stands in Waterloo Place on a granite column by Benjamin Dean Wyatt. Nelson's Column, erected in Trafalgar Square in 1843, supports a statue by E H Bailey of the hero of Trafalgar. Again, Wellington presided over the plans for the memorial, combining the statue with a column designed by William Railton. A less martial statue was unveiled at the south end of Park Lane in 1880, to Lord Byron. The bronze statue by Charles Belt shows the poet with his dog, Bo'sun.

Memorials to more recent conflicts have joined the Wellington Statue and Arch around the Hyde Park Corner traffic island. Two First World War memorials were erected in 1925: the Royal Artillery Memorial, designed by Charles Sargeant Jagger and Lionel Pearson, and the Machine Gun Corps Memorial by Francis Derwent Wood. The Memorial Gates, designed by Liam O'Connor and erected at the top of Constitution Hill in 2002, honour troops from Africa, the Caribbean and the Indian sub-continent, while the Australian war memorial of 2003, designed by Janet Laurence, commemorates losses in both world wars.

Above: Copy of Raphael's Christ Carrying the Cross (now in the Prado, Madrid) by Féréol Bonnemaison, commissioned by Wellington when the original was in Paris between 1813 and 1818 (on loan from the Duke of Wellington's family)
Right: Adam's original design for the chimneypiece, about 1775 (Sir John Soane's Museum)

5 THE PORTICO DRAWING ROOM

This room takes its present name from the Corinthian portico added to the exterior of the house in 1828, when Benjamin Dean Wyatt encased the brick building in Bath stone. Identified by Adam as the '2nd Drawing Room', this room was originally designed to make the most of the house's exceptional setting. Before Wellington and Wyatt added on the Waterloo Gallery, the wall facing the fireplace would have afforded a fine prospect out across Hyde Park from three windows. Facing west, the room would have been filled with sunlight in the afternoon and, as the south wall was solid, none of the noise from Piccadilly would have intruded on the illusion of a country-house saloon. At night, candlelight shone from gilded candelabra on torchères decorated with seated griffin, designed to match the pier glasses (which are today on loan from the Duke of Wellington's family). The tall windows under the portico were only created in 1828, together with the vast pier glasses, to compensate for the removal of the windows in the west wall, when the Waterloo Gallery was installed.

A further clue to the character of the original room can be found in the fine marble chimneypiece, which was probably carved by John Deval the Younger (1728–94). Adam's design includes an ornament of stags, a quote from the coat of arms of his patron Baron Apsley, later 2nd Earl of Bathurst. The actual chimneypiece is decorated with a frieze of Cupid and Psyche, and with symbols of seduction: a quiver of Cupid's arrows crossed with a flaming torch of passion. This romantic theme continues in Adam's surviving ceiling and frieze, and suggests that he may originally have intended this room as a ladies' drawing room. The pier glasses, overmantel and pier tables were designed for the room by Wyatt and four more 'handsome carved and gilt tables', possibly also designed by Wyatt, are mentioned in the earliest known inventory of the room, drawn up in 1854. These side tables would have given the room a more formal character.

The present colour scheme, hangings, curtains and carpet date from 1978 and 1995 and are a re-creation by the Victoria & Albert Museum of the decoration as it survived in 1852. Paintings in the room from the duke's day include portraits of prime ministers (Pitt the Younger and Spencer

1515

NAPOLEON BONAPARTE (1769-1821)
ROBERT LEFEVRE ((1756-1830)
W.M.1515-1845.

erceval), Napoleon and Marshal Soult, the leader of the French forces against Wellington in Spain. A ortrait of Charles Arbuthnot (1767–1850), also ung in this room by Wellington, commemorates he 15 years during which the two men resided ogether at Apsley House. Wellington was an rdent admirer of his friend's wife, Harriet rbuthnot, and after her sudden death in 1834, ged 40, from cholera, Wellington invited Charles o live out his days at Apsley House. The large opies after Raphael (on loan from the Duke of Wellington's family) were commissioned by the st Duke when he was in Paris, as Commander-n-Chief of the Allied Armies of Occupation in France, from the chief conservator at the Louvre, Féréol Bonnemaison. Wellington ensured the safe return of the original paintings to the Prado in Madrid, together with other masterpieces from conquered countries that Napoleon had sought to keep in Paris. The magnificent pair of Sèvres porcelain vases, made in 1814, are recorded in this room in 1853. They are decorated with a quagga and a gnu, animals copied from Samuel Daniell's engravings of African scenery and animals published in 1804. Each vase stands on an ormolu (gilt bronze) foot by the celebrated goldsmith Pierre-Philippe Thomire (1751–1843).

Above left: Napoleon *Bonaparte (1769–1821), a copy after Gérard*
Above: A pair of torchères *made to Adam's design for the Portico Drawing Room (private collection)*

THE WATERLOO GALLERY

Stepping through Wyatt's doorway from the Portico Drawing Room, visitors discover one of the great palatial interiors of Britain. More than 28m (90ft) long, the magnificent gallery fills two storeys and stretches beyond the back of the original house by two window bays in its own extension built between 1828 and 1829.

The Duke of Wellington had several reasons for creating such an impressive space. The main purpose of the gallery may have been to accommodate the Waterloo Banquet, an annual dinner held at Apsley House to celebrate the defeat of Napoleon. In the early years, before the Waterloo Gallery was created, Wellington hosted a select gathering; in 1821, for example, the guest list included King George IV, most of the royal dukes and foreign ambassadors, and Wellington's own generals who had fought with him at Waterloo. Rather than see the numbers of veteran generals dwindle with the passing years, Wellington expanded his guest list to include those younger officers present at the battle who later rose to the same rank. The Waterloo Gallery could seat 85 for ceremonial banquets. King William IV was guest of honour in 1830 and the dinner continued annually until the duke's death in 1852.

The Waterloo Gallery also raised Apsley House from an aristocratic town house to palatial status, befitting the foreign princes and politicians the duke received here. The architectural style of the room evokes the age of King Louis XIV of France, in preference to the Greek Revival that succeeded Adam's influence, the French Empire style favoured by Napoleon, or the Egyptian revival that followed Napoleon's campaign to the Nile. The windows in the Waterloo Gallery have sliding shutters fitted with mirrors, which can be pulled across the windows at night. The light from the torchères and central chandelier would have flickered over gilded decoration and silk hangings, reflected by the mirrored shutters, creating an evocation of Louis XIV's Versailles and its celebrated mirrored room known as the *Galerie des Glaces* (created between 1678 and 1685 by the French architect J H Mansart). Wellington must have wished to share with his guests some of the splendours of the *ancien régime*, befitting his title as Prince of Waterloo and his position as

a former Commander of the Allied Forces of Occupation in France, responsible for restoring Louis XVIII to the French throne. But the Waterloo Gallery gives only a pale reflection of Wellington's ambitious architectural plans. He had been expected to build at Stratfield Saye a magnificent Waterloo Palace, the 19th century's answer to Blenheim (the palace created by Sir John Vanbrugh from 1705 for the 1st Duke of Marlborough as a national gift after his victory over the army of King Louis XIV of France). But Wellington must have realised that the building and upkeep of a Waterloo Palace would have ruined him and his heirs, and so restricted himself to remodelling Apsley House. His country residence at Stratfield Saye in Hampshire proved adequate for his needs.

Many details in the Waterloo Gallery, including the gilded overdoors, were designed by the duke's close friend, Mrs Arbuthnot. She was asked to intervene in November 1828, when relations between Wellington and Wyatt became strained. But not even she had the final say, as she noted in her journal on 11 February 1830, 'I am rather discontented, however, for I think he is going to spoil his gallery &, as I took infinite trouble about it, it vexes me … He is going to hang it with yellow damask, which is just the very worst colour he can have for pictures & will kill the effect of the gilding. However, he will have it.'

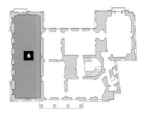

Left: View of the Waterloo Gallery today, showing the gilded overdoors designed by Mrs Arbuthnot
Below: A painting of the Waterloo Gallery in 1852 by Joseph Nash, which records the denser arrangement of paintings and the yellow silk damask covering the walls at that time (Victoria & Albert Museum)

*Right: The Egg Dance:
Peasants Merrymaking
in an Inn, painted in about
1670 by Jan Steen
(1625 or 1626–79)*

Wellington did indeed have his way: the yellow damask was hung in March 1830. It seems unlikely that the yellow clashed with the paintings given the density of the duke's arrangement. As he hung over 130 paintings in the room (almost double the 70 here today) they would have been as closely packed as the paintings in the Piccadilly Drawing Room today. The 1st Duke was simply following the Regency taste for yellow walls. He would have seen gilding and yellow silk used together in India and Russia and had chosen it for three other rooms in this suite. The effect of the yellow wall-coverings in the Waterloo Gallery is recorded in a watercolour painted by Joseph Nash in 1852 (see page 17). Nevertheless, the 2nd Duke of Wellington replaced the yellow silk damask with red almost immediately after his father's death.

Nash's painting also shows the two vast torchères, made of grey Siberian (Korgon) porphyry. They were originally intended for the Winter Palace in St Petersburg but were presented to the duke in 1826 by Tsar Nicholas I of Russia. For the Waterloo Banquet the tables were assembled around them, and the two vases of Swedish porphyry were dressed with flowers. These vases were presented by King Charles John XIV of Sweden and are on loan from the Duke of Wellington's family. Nash's watercolour also shows a bordered carpet, described in an inventory of 1854 as 'a large cut pile carpet to centre of room'; together with 'a ditto a size smaller for each end'.

A painting by William Salter (on loan from the Duke of Wellington's family) records the gallery in use for the Waterloo Banquet of 1836. It shows Wellington proposing the loyal toast, prior to the Grenadier Guards playing the national anthem and the guests settling into dessert. The women of the party appear only in the doorway – they were not present during the banquet but were admitted for the speeches.

The Spanish Royal Collection

The President of the Royal Academy thought the Correggio was worth fighting a battle for, and that it should be framed in diamonds.

The Waterloo Gallery provided a fitting home for most of the 165 paintings from the Spanish Royal Collection. They had been discovered after the Battle of Vitoria in 1813 in the abandoned baggage carriage of Joseph Bonaparte, brother of Napoleon and at that time king of Spain. The Duke of Wellington was given the paintings by King Ferdinand VII of Spain in 1816.

Acquired as rolled-up canvases, the paintings gradually covered the walls as more and more were conserved and framed each year. Most of the works are relatively small for a gallery of this scale, suggesting that the departing king's hurried selection must have been influenced by their portability.

The greatest masterpieces in the collection today are four paintings by Diego Velázquez (1599–1660): *The Waterseller of Seville*; *Two Young Men Eating at a Humble Table*; *A Spanish Gentleman, probably José Nieto* and *Pope Innocent X*, together with *The Agony in the Garden* by Correggio (about 1494–1534). The President of the Royal Academy, Benjamin West, thought the Correggio was worth fighting a battle for, and that it should be framed in diamonds.

Wellington had all the paintings framed in the rococo-revival taste appropriate to the room. He had a special frame made for his favourite painting, the Correggio, with a locking glass window on hinges. Wellington kept the key in his pocket and would lend it to no one. He was apparently in the habit of raising the window to dust the painting with his own handkerchief.

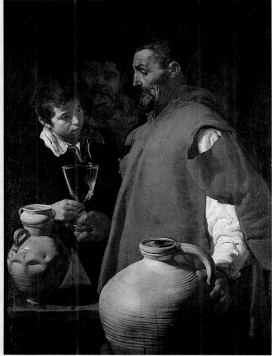

Above: The Agony in the Garden by Antonio Allegri, known as Correggio, painted in about 1525 (detail)
Right: The Waterseller of Seville by Diego Velázquez, painted in about 1620 (detail)
Far right: A portrait of Pope Innocent X by Diego Velázquez, painted in about 1620 (detail)

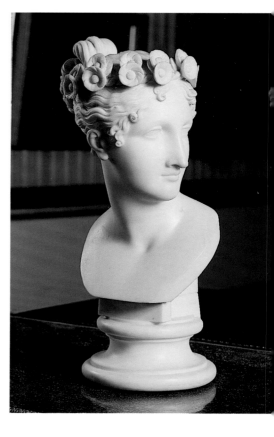

Above left: Adam's design for Lady Bathurst's watch case (Sir John Soane's Museum)
Above right: Head of a Dancer, a marble bust by Antonio Canova, given by the sculptor to Wellington in 1817

7 THE YELLOW DRAWING ROOM

The second door in the Waterloo Gallery leads back into the original house, built by Adam. In Adam's plan this room is called simply the '3rd Drawing Room or Toilet Room'. His original marble fireplace still survives, together with some of his designs for the fittings and furnishings of the room, including one drawing for a table frame and top and another for an exquisite watch case for Lady Bathurst, a personal trophy to fashion where her watch could luxuriate overnight. In the 1st Duke's day this room was used as a drawing room. By 1854 furnishings included a 'Grecian Couch in white and gold', 11 chairs, four footstools, a writing table, a sofa table, lamps and six stuffed birds on a stand. Striped 'tabaret' silk decorated the walls, with amber silk damask curtains. The present decoration is a reconstruction from 1994.

The bust by Antonio Canova (on the pier table) was a gift to Wellington from the sculptor in 1817. It is one of four 'ideal' heads presented by Canova to the British gentlemen who were instrumental in returning to Rome treasures looted by Napoleon for the Louvre. Canova had begun the repatriation of such booty by requesting the return of the Papal archives to the Vatican, so that daily business might continue. As Commander of the Allied Armies of Occupation in France, Wellington was forced to begin a more widescale denuding of the 'Musée Napoleon' after the king of the Netherlands decided to send his troops into the Louvre to recover his country's stolen masterpieces.

8 THE STRIPED DRAWING ROOM

In the original house designed by Robert Adam, a dressing room, a servant's room and a bedroom completed the circuit of fine rooms on the first floor. Wyatt combined these three rooms to make the present Striped Drawing Room at the same time as the addition in 1820 of the State Dining Room that lies beyond, thus providing Wellington with a room where his guests could relax, before or after dinner, and where the duke could also display his growing collection of portraits. Card tables covered with green cloth were provided, for playing loo and écarté, together with a board for draughts and backgammon, ivory dice boxes and table lamps.

This room also became a personal hall of fame to Wellington's military friends and might have been inspired by his visit to St Petersburg in 1826, where he would have seen the gallery that Tsar Nicholas I was building in his Winter Palace for portraits of heroes of the Napoleonic War. The three full-length portraits by Thomas Lawrence, still on display in the room today, were planned as part of a series, but after the artist died the duke had to resort to buying pictures by other artists to complete his gallery of military heroes.

The distinctive character of the interior comes from the striped hangings and furniture, originally installed in 1826 (the current hangings are reproductions). Here Wyatt and Wellington might have been inspired by the celebrated tent room in Napoleon's apartment at Malmaison, the house decorated between 1800 and 1802 for Josephine Bonaparte by architects Charles Percier and P-F-L Fontaine. Describing the effect of the room in 1853, as well as the portraits of politicians and of Napoleon in the Portico Drawing Room, the *Quarterly Review* likened it to a 'private Valhalla', the heavenly hall of Viking mythology where the bravest warriors were immortalised.

Above: The Striped Drawing Room painted in 1852 by Thomas Shotter Boys (1803–74) (Victoria & Albert Museum)
Left: Sir Thomas Lawrence's portrait of Henry William Paget, 1st Marquess of Anglesey, who served with Wellington at Waterloo

To accompany the portraits of his friends, Wellington bought the panoramic painting, *The Battle of Waterloo* (1843) by Sir William Allan (1782–1850) (illustrated on pages 32–3). When Wellington saw this painting exhibited at the Royal Academy he remarked, 'Good, not too much smoke,' and reserved it for his collection. Today it still hangs where he left it, as recorded in a watercolour of the room painted by Thomas Shotter Boys in 1852.

The painting shows the battle from the point of view of the French Army, at 7.30pm on 18 June 1815. Napoleon can be seen in the foreground at the right of the picture, mounted on his white charger, while Wellington is a tiny figure in the middle distance to the left, on his faithful chestnut, Copenhagen. At this stage in the battle, things had begun to swing against the French forces, despite their numerical superiority to the combined British, Prussian, Dutch and Belgian troops, jointly commanded by Wellington and the Prussian general, Prince von Blücher. This was Napoleon's last offensive, when he sent five of his battalions against the centre of the allied position. But the battle was to last for only another half hour, ending in a massive rout of the French troops. Although Wellington displayed his usual sangfroid during the battle, he admitted afterwards, 'I never took so much trouble about any battle, and never was so near being beat'.

9 THE OCTAGON PASSAGE

This magical mirrored little room, linking the Striped Drawing Room to the State Dining Room, has its modest name recorded in a floor plan drawn up by Wellington's architect, Benjamin Dean Wyatt in about 1829. In Robert Adam's original plan the passage was not octagonal and led to a 'Powdering Room' and closet off the adjoining bedroom.

10 THE STATE DINING ROOM

This grand dining room was finished in 1819 by Benjamin Dean Wyatt. Up to this point, the duke and his guests had dined downstairs. Wellington built his new State Dining Room as part of a three-storey addition to the north-east of Apsley House. Below were the duke's apartments; above on the third storey, there were two bedrooms, all linked by new back stairs.

The State Dining Room was the setting for the great annual Waterloo Banquet from 1820 until the completion of the Waterloo Gallery ten years later. On its inauguration, this dining room must have seemed the ultimate expression of Wellington's ambitions to entertain in style. The arrangement of the room today gives some impression of the magnificence of the Waterloo Banquet.

The glittering centrepiece on display here today is part of a silver and silver-gilt service presented to Wellington by the Portuguese Council of Regency in 1816, to commemorate victories over Napoleon in the Peninsular War (1808–14). In the centre, figures representing the four continents pay tribute to the united armies of Portugal, Britain and Spain while dancing nymphs encircle them. Battles are named on individual plaques. The full Portuguese Service comprises more than 1,000 pieces and was designed by the court painter Domingos António de Sequeira (1768–1857), and made at the artist's house from 1812 to 1816 by workers from the Military Arsenal at Lisbon.

An inventory also reveals that by 1854 this room had a carpet surrounded by an oil cloth (a forerunner of linoleum). Wellington would protect his carpets before the Waterloo Banquet by laying oil cloths and druggets (long woollen mats).

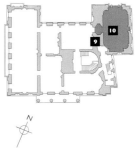

Left: View from the State Dining Room through to the Waterloo Gallery, with the silver and silver-gilt Portuguese centrepiece in the foreground

The Waterloo Shield

The glittering Waterloo Shield and Standard Candelabra, presented to Wellington by the merchants and bankers of London, were brought out for the annual Waterloo Banquet.

In 1822, the Merchants and Bankers of the City of London presented Wellington with a magnificent silver-gilt shield and a pair of candelabra to celebrate the victory at Waterloo, which had heralded a period of prosperity for the capital. The glittering Waterloo Shield was designed by Thomas Stothard in 1814 and made by Benjamin Smith; Smith also made the two Standard Candelabra between 1816 and 1817. The pieces were brought out for the annual Waterloo Banquet; when this took place in the State Dining Room they were displayed together on the sideboard. In 1822 James Deville invoiced the Duke for 'fixing in the Sideboard … a Large Brass Plate with a Revolving mechanical joint … to attach the whole to the Shield to allow it to incline as may be required and to Revolve Round'. The shield and candelabra were usually displayed in the Museum, where they can still be seen today.

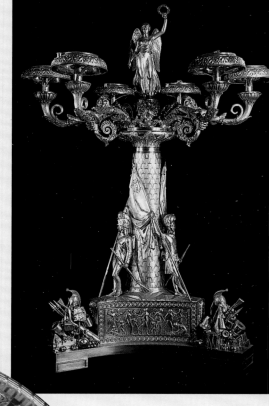

Above: One of the pair of Standard Candelabra, with three supporting figures representing an English, Scottish and Irish soldier
Left: The Waterloo Shield, inspired by the Shield of Achilles described by Homer in the Iliad, shows Wellington in the central group with the 10 major battles from the Peninsular Campaign depicted in the surrounding reliefs

The State Dining Room, was made for more than reunions of Waterloo veterans. With its state portraits, presented by the sitters themselves, it embodies Wellington's unique social position as the friend and near-equal of the crowned heads of Europe.

As Allied Commander, and a ready diplomat fluent in French, Wellington held a position that today might be equivalent to combining the duties of the commander of NATO with those of a roving ambassador. Yet however much he was revered and fêted abroad, back home in the decade after Waterloo Wellington had no obvious role to play. His spell as Prime Minister (1828–30) proved how much his absence on military campaigns had left him out of step with the times and with growing calls for constitutional change.

Consciously or otherwise, Wellington seems to have created for himself in this almost windowless room a closed world commemorating old friends and the old order. Tact or modesty may have made it necessary to create the impression, preserved to this day, that the State Dining Room, and later the Waterloo Gallery, were created simply for an annual reunion of Wellington's comrades-in-arms from Waterloo, as if he had no greater guests or political agenda.

At the dinner table Wellington was reputedly an excellent host, putting his guests at ease with many humorous anecdotes. Walter Scott was surprised at his conversation, at 'the sweetness & abandon with which it flowed'. Wellington showed no interest in fine wines or food, however, eating little and swiftly, his favourite dishes being mincemeat, rice, or roast saddle of mutton with salad. To the frustration of his French chef, Wellington would simply return the proposed menu for the day without discussion, after scrawling across the bottom 'pudding and tart', to satisfy the demands of his sweet tooth.

 THE SLIP PASSAGE

Leaving the Dining Room through the service door to the right of the sideboard, visitors enter the Slip Passage, which leads back to the Piccadilly Drawing Room. Behind the curved door from the Dining Room lies another room (closed to visitors) that may have contained a water-closet for the convenience of dinner guests. The inventory of 1854 records dining tables stored in this passage ('2 butler tray stands' and 'Sundry deal tops and tressels used for the Gallery') with the floor covered by a fitted oil cloth to catch the spills. The cabinets are a modern addition to display pieces from the silver Portuguese Service. The tour continues downstairs in the museum.

Left: *The State Dining Room painted by Thomas Shotter Boys (1803–74) in 1852 (Victoria & Albert Museum)*

☑ THE MUSEUM

After Waterloo Wellington was showered with gifts by monarchs grateful to him for saving their thrones from Napoleon. At Apsley House the duke created a private treasury, called the 'museum', off the entrance hall to store and show to visitors these gifts. This was not a permanent display, for the silver and porcelain services and presentation plate came and went, dressing the tables of brilliant banquets hosted by Wellington upstairs.

The present room is the museum's third location. Initially it stood on the site of the present entrance hall. When the west wing containing the Waterloo Gallery was added to the house between 1828 and 1830, the collection moved to the new sitting room beneath the gallery, at the north end of the wing, as recorded in two watercolours by Thomas Shotter Boys. The 2nd Duke of Wellington moved the museum to its present position after his father's death in 1852, presumably in order to place it closer to the entrance for visitors. Shotter Boys recorded this arrangement in a watercolour of 1853 (see page 46). The objects on display also proved inspiring for the Duchess of Wellington, who drew solace from the collection during her last illness. During a visit to Apsley House on 24 April 1831, the novelist Maria Edgeworth encountered the duchess lying on a sofa admiring the trophies. The duchess apparently 'exclaimed with weak-voiced enthusiasm, "All tributes to merit! There's the value; all pure, no corruption ever suspected even."' This is a touching testimonial from a woman who spent much of her married life apart from her husband.

The most eye-catching piece in the collection is the massive, glittering Waterloo Shield in its custom-built rosewood showcase (designed by Wyatt and Wellington), flanked by the Standard Candelabra (see page 24). These magnificent presentation pieces in gilded silver were intended for display together, blazing from the sideboard at the annual Waterloo Banquet. The case still contains the original mechanism by which the shield and candelabra can be rotated at the turn of a handle. After the shield and candelabra, the finest plate includes two silver-gilt centrepieces made by Paul Storr between 1810 and 1812 and the silver-gilt Waterloo Vase designed by Thomas Stothard and made between 1824 and 1825, each presented to Wellington by noblemen, gentlemen and officers.

The porcelain on display nearly all dates from one decade, from about 1810 to 1820, and is of the highest quality. The Egyptian Service, displayed in the central case, was originally commissioned for Josephine Bonaparte in 1809 to mark her divorce from Napoleon, but she rejected the gift in 1812. In 1818 King Louis XVIII of France presented the service to Wellington. The service was designed by Jean Charles Nicolas Brachard of the Sèvres porcelain factory. The designs for the 66 plates and other pieces were taken from illustrations of ancient Egyptian monuments in the celebrated book, *Voyage dans la basse et la haute Egypte*, published in 1802 by Dominique Vivant Denon (1747–1825), following Napoleon's invasion of Egypt. In Wellington's own day, the Egyptian Service was kept in store.

The Prussian Service, displayed in cases on the south and east walls, presents Wellington's life and military campaigns in scenes painted on 64 dessert plates, as well as vases, ice-buckets,

Above: Three plates on display in the Museum, from the Saxon Service (top and bottom) and the Prussian Service (middle), depicting Apsley House before the extensive remodelling by the 1st Duke and Benjamin Dean Wyatt

Right: A fruit stand in the form of a figure from the Egyptian Service

Facing page: Batons presented to Wellington between 1809 and 1844 as commander of the victorious armies of Europe

ice-cream pails and cups, fruit platters, sauce-boats, soup tureens and wine coolers. Made by the Berlin porcelain factory from 1816 to 1819, the service was presented to the duke by King Frederick William III of Prussia. The green porcelain obelisk, decorated with Wellington's titles and orders and flanked by white porcelain river gods, is one of 292 pieces from the service currently at Apsley House.

The Saxon Service was made from 1818 by the Meissen porcelain factory and presented to Wellington in 1819 by King Frederick Augustus IV of Saxony. Among 105 hand-painted dessert plates, two show views of Apsley House as it originally appeared, built in brick by Robert Adam (another plate depicting the house can be seen in the Prussian Service). The others are painted with scenes of battles and other views from the Napoleonic Wars. Only a selection from the service can be displayed; it also includes vases and sauce-boats.

The Austrian Service, the last great production of the Vienna porcelain factory, was presented by Emperor Francis II of Austria in 1820. The

collection also includes 44 dessert plates in *gros bleu* Sèvres porcelain, painted in 1821–2 and presented by King Louis XVIII of France in 1823.

Other notable objects in the collection include 17 presentation boxes and a collection of 13 gold and silver swords, some used by the duke (including his sword from the Battle of Waterloo) and some captured from his opponents including the Indian leader Tipu Sultan of Mysore, and Napoleon himself. Napoleon's sword, made by his goldsmith Martin-Guillaume Biennais in about 1809, is displayed with a choice of three scabbards. It was intended for Napoleon's triumphal entry into Brussels but, legend has it, the sword was taken by a Prussian from Napoleon's carriage at Waterloo as he fled out the opposite door. The batons were presented to Wellington as commander of various European armies. Of the field marshal's batons, three are British, one Portuguese, one Hanoverian, one Dutch, one Spanish, one Austrian and one Prussian. They are accompanied by Wellington's staff as High Constable of England.

The tour continues in the basement.

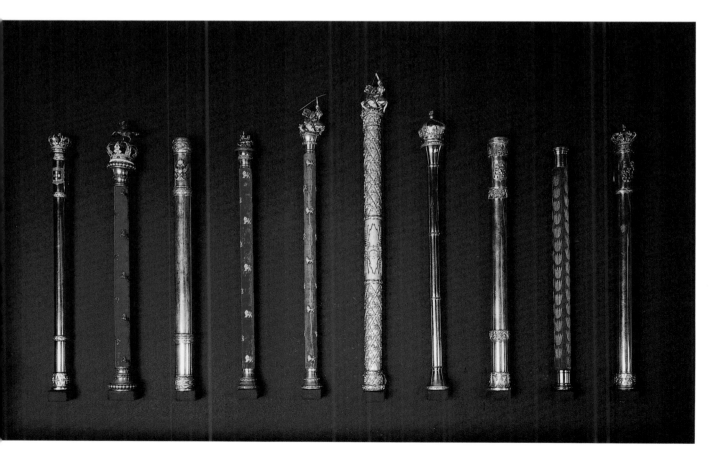

Right: A painting of 1840 by Andrew Morton (1802–45) showing Wellington in his library on the ground floor with his Private Secretary, John Gurwood (Wallace Collection)

THE BASEMENT AND SERVANTS' QUARTERS

The basement of Apsley House was the domain of the servants, but it also accommodated ample stables and a coach house. A census of 1851 provides a glimpse of life below stairs, recording 13 male and eight female servants, including the steward (or butler), the housekeeper, two porters, two under-butlers, one footman, four housemaids, two kitchen maids, a stillroom maid, two coachmen, one groom and four 'helpers' in the stables (the cook is not recorded, so must have been away at the time of the census).

A floor plan from 1904 records more than 30 rooms within the basement, from kitchen, scullery, larder, wine cellars, coal cellar and servants' hall to a carpenter's workshop and a large muniment room in which documents would have been archived. There was also a strongroom for the silver and silver-gilt dining services. At the centre of the basement a service staircase, opposite the principal stairs, ascends the full height of the house. This was the main thoroughfare for servants (who were expected to remain invisible to visitors), and also led to attic bedrooms where the under-servants slept, two or three to a room.

Wellington had his horses stabled at basement level, on the east side of the house. A steep ramp led down from a ground-floor stable block (now demolished) at the east end of the forecourt, to the Stables Court. At basement level, stables and a coach house were provided, while accommodation for grooms and coachmen occupied the ground floor. As the *Quarterly Review* noted in 1853, 'this basement-level courtyard proved particularly convenient for Wellington as he was able to mount and dismount, enter or leave a carriage, in secure privacy, free from the attentions of admirers and protesters'.

The main part of the basement open to visitors today is the former Steward's Room. It is last recorded as such in a state of abandoned disarray, in a photograph taken in October 1949 (see facing page, below). Other photographs taken at this time record a kitchen and secondary kitchen, a vegetable kitchen, a pastry kitchen and a servants' hall. The kitchen equipment was removed to the Museum of London shortly before Apsley House first opened as the Wellington Museum in 1952. At that time no plans were made for showing the servants' quarters to the public.

PRIVATE ROOMS

The Wellington Museum Act of 1947, by which the 7th Duke gave the house and contents to the nation, reserved parts of the basement and the ground floor and all of the two top storeys for the Duke of Wellington and his family. They continue to live at Apsley House in these private apartments.

These rooms are not open to visitors, but their appearance in the 1st Duke's day is recorded in detailed descriptions and illustrations published in 1853, on the occasion of the first public opening by the 2nd Duke of Wellington. The thorough account of these rooms given by Richard Ford in the *Quarterly Review* in 1853 also appeared as the introduction to Ford's book *Apsley House and Walmer Castle* (London 1853) with illustrations taken from the watercolours of the interiors of the house specially commissioned from the artist Thomas Shotter Boys. These give a vivid picture of the house as it was arranged at about the time of the 1st Duke's death.

Left: The 1st Duke's study shown in a lithograph published in Richard Ford's book, Apsley House and Walmer Castle (London 1853)
Below: The Steward's Room, photographed in 1949, long after domestic life at Apsley House had been interrupted by the Second World War

History of
the Iron Duke

By the time of his death in 1852,
Wellington, the Iron Duke, was a
national hero. Some 200,000 people
queued to see his body lying in
state, before a spectacular funeral
that concluded with his burial at
St Paul's Cathedral. The following
year his son opened Apsley House
to the public and newspapers called
for the house to be preserved intact
as a shrine to Britain's greatest
general. But it is hard to detect any
promise of this future glory in
Wellington's early life.

READING THE HISTORY

*This section describes the history and career of Arthur
Wellesley, 1st Duke of Wellington. There are special
features on Wellington's reputation as a ladies' man
(page 34) and his domestic habits (page 37).
The history of Apsley House is covered in a separate
section, beginning on page 38.*

EARLY YEARS

Born in Dublin in 1769, the fourth son of the 1st Earl of Mornington, Arthur Wesley did not make a promising start. His father died when he was 12, and the same year he was sent to Eton, together with his younger brother Gerald. After three years, it was clear that Arthur was not doing well and his mother removed him from Eton, concluding that her 'ugly boy Arthur' was only good for cannon-fodder, or, as she put it, 'fit food for powder'. After she moved to Brussels in 1785, she enrolled Arthur in the *Ecole d'equitation,* a military academy at Angers in France. Here Arthur gained his life-long fluency in French. On leaving, his military career advanced, as was the custom, through the purchase of positions in regiments and he also entered the political arena as Member of the Irish Parliament for the constituency of Trim, from 1790 to 1795. By this time the family had changed their surname back to Wellesley, its 17th-century spelling.

THE NAPOLEONIC WARS

Arthur Wellesley began his military career at a turbulent time in Europe. Instability had increased in the wake of the French Revolution of 1789, and in 1793 Napoleon led France to war against the British and their allies. Arthur saw his first action in the Netherlands in 1794, earning an official commendation for his part in an engagement against the French. In 1796, as a colonel, he sailed for India, another theatre of British military operations, discovering on the way that his brother had been offered an appointment as Governor General there. India was the making of Arthur as a military commander and civic administrator. In 1804, at the age of only 34, he achieved a victory that he would later consider his best battle, over the confederation of Maratha states at Assaye.

Returning to England in 1805, he was elected to Parliament the following year and appointed Irish Secretary. He also married, in 1806, Lady Catherine ('Kitty') Pakenham, daughter of Edward, 2nd Baron Longford. Arthur had known her in Ireland during the early years of his military career and had in fact proposed to her in 1793, when her family had put an end to the affair, disapproving of his lowly prospects. It seems that Kitty had considered the engagement

Left: The great portrait of Wellington by Francisco de Goya (1746–1828); Goya completed the painting in 1812 but altered it in 1814 to show the extra honours his sitter had by then received (National Gallery, London) Below: A pair of Wellington boots designed and worn by the duke himself, now at Walmer Castle

Facing page: The Duke of Wellington looking at a bust of Napoleon by Charles Robert Leslie (1794–1859), c.1845

dissolved, but a mutual friend of the couple pressed Arthur to renew his proposals. Only a very strong sense of honour could have induced a notorious ladies' man, as Arthur already was, to agree to marry a woman he had not set eyes on for almost ten years. Apparently he regretted the match almost immediately, remarking to his brother at their wedding, 'She has grown ugly, by Jove!' It was not an easy marriage.

By 1807, Britain was in the middle of another military crisis. Napoleon had already defeated the Austrians, Russians and Prussians and Britain alone continued to hold out, having defeated the combined French and Spanish fleets at Trafalgar in 1805. Arthur Wellesley sailed for Denmark in 1807, to serve in an expedition against the Danish, culminating in the siege of Copenhagen. He performed creditably, and he was promoted to lieutenant-general and given command of 9,000 men when war with Napoleon flared up in Spain in 1808. This was the start of the Peninsular War (1808–14), triggered by a Spanish revolt against Napoleon when he deposed the King of Spain in favour of his brother, Joseph.

Above: The Battle of
Waterloo, painted in 1843
by Sir William Allan

Facing page: Some of
Wellington's battle orders
from the Battle of Waterloo
(private collection)

THE PENINSULAR WAR

Supported by the Spanish and Portuguese armies, the British troops had mixed fortunes in the Peninsular War, although Wellesley himself had some notable successes and was raised to the peerage as Baron Douro of Wellesley and Viscount Wellington of Talavera in 1809. For his capture of Ciudad Rodrigo in 1812 he was rewarded by Spain with the title of Duke of Ciudad Rodrigo and, following further successes that year, was appointed as generalissimo of the Spanish armies. Parliament rewarded him with a grant of £100,000; he was also elevated to Marquess (August 1812) and awarded the Order of the Garter (March 1813).

The campaign of 1813 saw the French driven out of Spain and Wellington's advance into France.

After his victory at the Battle of Vitoria on 21 June 1813, Wellington was promoted to field marshal. Two days after facing Marshal Soult at the Battle of Toulouse (10 April 1814) Wellington learnt that Napoleon had abdicated. He returned to England, after an absence of six years, and was created Marquess of Douro and Duke of Wellington, with a further grant voted by the House of Commons of £400,000. Six weeks later he was back in France as ambassador, and took up residence in Paris.

THE WATERLOO CAMPAIGN

Napoleon's escape from exile on the Island of Elba obliged Wellington to resume his military career, and in March 1815 he was appointed

Commander of the Anglo-Netherland and Hanoverian forces in Europe. Napoleon set out to defeat Field Marshal Prince von Blücher's Prussian army and then overcome Wellington's allied forces (only about a third of whom were British) before the Austrians and Russians could reach Belgium. Despite suffering heavy losses, Blücher withstood Napoleon's Grand Army at Quatre Bras on 16 June. Wellington fell back to Waterloo, to fields he had earlier identified as ideal terrain for his troops.

Not appreciating the care with which Wellington had planned his battle, Napoleon confidently launched his main attack at 1pm on 18 June, pounding the allied troops with a series of massive but uncoordinated assaults. Wellington paced the battle carefully, expecting the arrival of the Prussian forces late in the day. When they did finally arrive in the early evening, Wellington still had 35,000 men standing; the French army was decisively routed. Napoleon withdrew to Paris, having lost about half his army, and abdicated four days later. For all the celebrations, Wellington knew that the Battle of Waterloo had been a very close call indeed. About 24,000 allied troops had fallen, alongside a French toll of 26,000 dead and another 10,000 missing. He famously wrote to a friend the following day:

'Next to a battle lost, the greatest misery is a battle gained.'

The display of his collections at Apsley House could be seen as a way of consolidating his victory.

The Ladies' Man

During his residence in Paris after the fall of Napoleon, female admiration for Wellington became a craze known as *la nouvelle religion*.

Throughout his life, Arthur Wellesley had a weakness for intimate conversation and correspondence with women that left him open to accusations of affairs, some of which were well-founded. Trim, 5ft 9in tall, with aquiline features (his large hooked nose caused him to be known to his troops as 'Old Nosey') he had a way with words and many admirers. As his military career, spanning nearly 30 years, was spent abroad, he felt free to lead a bachelor life while Kitty raised their two sons in England. Unaffected and short-sighted, Kitty had none of the requisite skills of a society hostess and preferred to stay at their Hampshire home, where she could dress simply in muslin with no make-up. When she took to asking their servants about the duke's movements he warned her in writing, 'If it goes on I must live somewhere else'. Nevertheless, Kitty worshipped her hero from afar and they were reconciled by the time of her death at Apsley House in 1831.

Wellington's increasing celebrity only swelled his reputation as a ladies' man. During his residence in Paris after the fall of Napoleon, female admiration for Wellington became a craze known as *la nouvelle religion*. He is known to have escorted Napoleon's former mistress Giuseppina Grassini, and the French actress Mlle George, also a former lover of Napoleon, is reputed to have said that 'the duke was by far the more vigorous'. His principal female admirers in London were Lady Jersey, Lady Shelley and Harriet Arbuthnot. They competed for his attention, a sport recorded in popular caricature engravings. Wellington admired Mrs Arbuthnot in particular for her social graces and her mind for politics. The unfounded tradition that they were lovers dates from the publication in 1887 of the diary of Charles Greville, who took revenge on the duke for having an affair in about 1820 with his mother, Lady Charlotte Greville.

But Wellington's sincerest admiration was reserved for his elder daughter-in-law, Lady Douro, whose portrait hung prominently at Apsley House. Despite a lifetime of female adulation, he remained convinced that 'no woman ever loved me; never in my whole life'.

Above: Joseph Nollekens's bust of the duke, 1813, considered by Wellington's family to be the best likeness of him
Right, top: The Duchess of Wellington, engraving from a drawing by Thomas Lawrence
Right, above: Harriet Arbuthnot, engraving after a portrait by Thomas Lawrence
Right: A fictional account of the adventures of the Duke of Wellington penned by the young, star-struck Charlotte Brontë (British Library)

WELLINGTONMANIA

After defeating Napoleon, Wellington returned to Paris as Commander of the Allied Armies of Occupation. Both Wellington and Napoleon were 46 years old when their military careers concluded at the Battle of Waterloo in 1815. Whereas Napoleon died in exile on the Isle of St Helena in 1821, aged 52, Wellington pursued a second career as a diplomat and statesman and remained in the public eye until his death in 1852, at the age of 83. More artists painted and sculpted Wellington than any other British sitter. Between 1795 and 1852 more than 200 likenesses were made by over 80 artists. He complained, 'I lament the fate of having passed my Manhood acquiring celebrity; and of having to pass my old Age in sitting for Busts and Artists, that they may profit by it'. Even so, Wellington kept a pile of engravings of himself by his desk to send to admirers. The insatiable public demand also saw his portrait on cuff links, snuff boxes, brooches, mugs and even door stops. Wellington's distinctive appearance, however, was also used to less flattering purposes in numerous caricatures satirising his political career.

WELLINGTON THE POLITICIAN

In 1818 Wellington entered the Cabinet as Master-General of the Ordnance and ten years later reluctantly accepted the position of Prime Minister. In 1829 he successfully steered through the Catholic Emancipation Bill, allowing Catholics to be admitted to Parliament and to hold any civil or municipal office, as well as most Crown offices. Wellington's other foreign and domestic policies, however, increasingly showed that he was out of touch with the times, and his government fell in November 1830. His opposition to the Reform Bill, which aimed to redistribute votes to the expanding industrial cities, was supremely unpopular and led to riots in London, during which the windows of Apsley House were twice smashed by protesters. Wellington installed iron shutters and high iron railings to protect his town house, and it is thought that this may have led to his enduring nickname, the Iron Duke. The first published instance of the ever-popular sobriquet occurs in an 1842 edition of the satirical magazine *Punch*, which described Wellington as 'the Wrought-iron Duke'.

Left: A martial caricature of the duke, entitled Portrait of a Noble Duke, 1829, artist unknown (Harris Museum and Art Galllery)
Below: Isaac Cruickshank's caricature of 1819, playing on Wellington's reputation as a ladies' man (British Museum)
Bottom: A political caricature of 1830 by William Heath, showing the duke facing an angry mob outside Apsley House (British Museum)

Right: The Duke of Wellington, painted by Francisco de Goya (1746–1828) in just three weeks after the Battle of Salamanca (22 July 1812), in order that the portrait of the liberator of Spain could be shown at the annual exhibition of the Academia de San Fernando in Madrid. Goya managed this by painting Wellington's head onto a composition he had already begun, probably of Joseph Bonaparte

THE FINAL YEARS

Wellington's final period in politics began in 1834 when he was returned as Foreign Secretary in Robert Peel's government. He was also appointed Chancellor of Oxford University in the same year. In the course of the following decade he held several important posts, including that of Commander-in-Chief of the army. He made a brief return to more active military duties in April 1848 when he was given responsibility for the defence of London, as Chartist rioting threatened to break out (although in the end this threat subsided). Throughout this period, Wellington continued to demonstrate the conservative views which had lost him public support, but by the time of his death, at Walmer Castle on 14 September 1852, his popularity had returned in full measure. He was given a state funeral and buried in St Paul's Cathedral, taking his place in history as Britain's greatest military commander.

Wellington at Home

With his military career over, Wellington's lifestyle was less itinerant, but he still moved between his own houses, and those of his friends, in a way that was not unusual for a leading member of Regency society. Apsley House was never intended to be his year-round residence. The same year it was purchased, Stratfield Saye in Hampshire was also acquired for Wellington. From January 1828 until December 1830, he served as Prime Minister and was able to live at 10 Downing Street while extending and remodelling Apsley House. From 1829, when he was appointed Lord Warden of the Cinque Ports, he also had the use of Walmer Castle on the Kent coast as his official residence.

Until his wife's death in 1831, Wellington tended to avoid Stratfield Saye, complaining to his friend Mrs Arbuthnot that his wife 'made his house so dull that nobody would go to it'. He had to be in London for Parliament, which met from January or early February until July. Occasional excursions for house parties, fox-hunting and shooting peppered the London season, but by midsummer society

removed to the countryside. In the autumn and winter Wellington would enjoy what he called 'a scamper about the country'. A regular house guest of Charles and Harriet Arbuthnot at Woodford Lodge in Northamptonshire, he once told his hosts that he regarded their house as his true home. On 7 September 1826 Mrs Arbuthnot noted in her journal, 'We are going to have a large party, larger than the house will well hold, & the Duke (who is always the person that makes the fewest difficulties) brings his own little travelling bed'.

The contrast between the grandeur of the reception rooms at Apsley House and the modest apartments in which he really lived, not only in London but also at Stratfield Saye and Walmer Castle, suggests that the old soldier was not at home in society salons. Nevertheless, there certainly was a time when 'the Beau' liked to entertain in style. At Apsley House in particular he created palatial reception rooms where he could live up to public expectations of a duke, and of the conqueror of Europe.

Right: A cartoon of Wellington by William Heath in 1829, graphically illustrating Wellington's well-known habit of taking his old camp bed between residences (Victoria & Albert Museum)
Far right, above: Walmer Castle, Wellington's residence from 1829, also in the care of English Heritage
Far right: Wellington's bedroom at Walmer Castle, with his camp bed still in place beside the chair in which he died

History of Apsley House

The brick town house built for Henry Bathurst, 1st Baron Apsley by Robert Adam bears little outward resemblance to the Apsley House of today; it was cased in Bath stone during extensive remodelling by Benjamin Dean Wyatt for the 1st Duke of Wellington. Only minor alterations have been made to the public rooms since the duke's day, but elements from both phases of the construction and decoration of Apsley House can still be seen.

READING THE HISTORY

This section describes the history of Apsley House from its building by Lord Apsley, through the changes made by the 1st Duke of Wellington, to the present day.

THE SETTING

Apsley House stands on Piccadilly, at the formal entrance to Hyde Park. To the south and east lie Buckingham Palace, with its walled gardens, and Green Park. In the 18th century, following the expansion of London from the City, these parks formed the western boundary of Westminster. The location is recorded in a watercolour of 1756, showing an apple stall at the park gates and an inn known as the Hercules Pillars. The location (according to Thomas Shepherd's popular guide, *London in the Nineteenth Century*, published in 1829) was 'one of the finest in the metropolis, standing at the very beginning of the town, entering westward and commanding fine views of the parks, with the Surrey and Kent hills in the distance'. At the junction of Knightsbridge and Piccadilly a turnpike with toll houses, established in 1726, marked the end of the open land surrounding the rural village of Kensington and the entry into the capital. The first of the houses on the north side of Piccadilly consequently became known as 'Number 1 London' (its actual address today is 149 Piccadilly).

THE FIRST HOUSE

The area grew fashionable with the development of Mayfair in the 1770s. Henry Bathurst (1714–94), who became Lord Chancellor and Baron Apsley in 1771, commissioned the architect Robert Adam (1728–92) to design and build Apsley House here the same year. By 1775, Henry had succeeded his father as 2nd Earl Bathurst, and acquired most of the land he needed for the house and its grounds, through several Crown

leases. Tradition holds that Bathurst forgot to buy out an apple seller, a widow named Mrs Allen (perhaps the woman in the 1756 watercolour), whose husband had built a cottage next to their stall. Allen's son claimed that the plot had been granted to his father by King George II for serving at the Battle of Dettingen (1743), and Bathurst only succeeded in buying the land in 1784. The brick-built house was completed at a cost of £10,000 in 1778, the year Bathurst left office. He is best known for building Apsley House: according to *The Dictionary of National Biography*, 'his abilities were mediocre and unsuited to the high offices which he came to fill'.

Apsley House is one of only three large central London houses both designed and furnished by Robert Adam (the others being 20 St James's Square, 1771–5, and Shelburne House, Berkeley Square, about 1762–7). Sir John Soane's Museum holds 59 of Adam's drawings for Apsley House, dated between 1771 and 1779. In 1778 Adam also produced a series of designs for a gateway to London at Hyde Park Corner, including a

tollhouse, weighbridge and pedestrian arches flanking the central road arch, with statues of the king and queen in niches. This grandiose structure would have stood west of Apsley House, but it was never constructed.

The house as built by Adam was recorded, in about 1816, on three dessert plates in the collection. These sources and Adam's original plan record a five-bay house, set back behind a forecourt with a small lodge at the west end. To the east, blank walls rose above a stable yard. To fit the irregular site Adam built an oval staircase, lit from above and screened by two columns from the passage that linked the entrance hall to the dining room at the back of the house; a private staircase directly opposite led to bedrooms on the second floor. Beyond lay the dining parlour with an octagonal dressing room, a closet, service stairs and a garden entrance filling the gap behind the stables. On the west side of the house was a library and a large drawing room. Upstairs, Adam provided a suite of three drawing rooms and a bedroom.

Above: Henry Bathurst, 1st Baron Apsley in his Lord Chancellor's robes, painted by George Dance (1741–1825) (Honourable Society of Lincoln's Inn)

Below: Robert Adam's design for the Portico Room ceiling at Apsley House, 6 April 1775 (Sir John Soane's Museum)

Below: View of Hyde Park Corner in about 1809, showing the turnpike gates with Apsley House on the left, by George Underwood (Sir John Soane's Museum)

Bottom: A fantasy of a new London palace for Wellington exhibited at the Royal Academy in 1816 by Joseph Gandy (private collection)

THE WELLESLEYS ARRIVE

Henry, 3rd Earl Bathurst (1762–1834), inherited the house from his father in 1794. A survey completed for him in 1796 records the stabling facilities to the east of the house: 'Stable yard three Coach-houses and Stables for nine Horses, with Servants Rooms over them'. In 1807, the 3rd Earl sold the lease of Apsley House for £16,000 to Wellington's older brother, Richard, Marquess Wellesley (1760–1842). Wellesley had been dismissed as Governor General of India, and he arrived back in England in 1806. Over the next two years he spent over £20,000 on new furniture and decorative schemes at Apsley House, eventually moving into the house in 1808 with his French wife Hyacinthe Gabrielle and their children. It was not an auspicious move: dreadful scenes ensued and the couple separated. Hyacinthe Gabrielle refused to leave Apsley House and Wellesley embarked on numerous affairs. In 1809 he went to Seville as Ambassador Extraordinary, returning to London – and his love affairs – as Foreign Secretary in 1810. In 1812, on the assassination of Spencer Perceval, Wellesley attempted to form a government, but was too unpopular to achieve it; he lost office and incurred substantial debts.

Partly to alleviate his brother's debts, in 1817 Wellington put in an anonymous offer to buy Apsley House for the generous sum of £40,000. Wellington had just returned from Paris where he had served in turn as Ambassador to the Court of France and as Commander of the Allied Armies of Occupation. For some of this time he had been living in the Palais Borghese, which still

erves as the British Embassy in Paris today. Wellington had bought the palace from Napoleon's sister Pauline, and now he needed a fashionable London town house to match.

WATERLOO PALACE

When he acquired Apsley House, Wellington did not have any grand plans to renovate it, as he was expected to commission a magnificent new Waterloo Palace. The house and estate at Stratfield Saye in Hampshire were bought in 1817 to be the site of the palace. Wellington's chosen architect for the project was Benjamin Dean Wyatt (1775–1852), but Wellington finally decided to limit future liabilities for himself and his heirs by expanding and remodelling Apsley House alone.

Wyatt's alterations to Apsley House were carried out in two main phases, almost a decade apart, and with quite a different feel to them. Between 1819 and 1820 Wyatt added a three-storey extension to the east, to provide a State Dining Room with new bedrooms and dressing rooms above and below. The annual Waterloo Banquet was held in this new dining room from 1820 until 1829.

This early work gives little indication of the full-blown Louis-revival style that Wyatt later developed for the Waterloo Gallery. The sober neo-Greek design of this early building campaign sought to sit comfortably alongside the earlier interiors of the original house. It has a masculine character appropriate to a military hero, in contrast to the more overtly princely pretensions of a decade later.

Above: Apsley House as built by Robert Adam, with the traffic of Hyde Park corner in the foreground, depicted in about 1816 on a dessert plate now on display in the Museum
Left: Apsley House in about 1853, as altered and enlarged by the 1st Duke of Wellington and Benjamin Dean Wyatt, overshadowed by the giant equestrian statue of Wellington opposite (see pages 12–13); detail, lithograph by Robert Carrick after a painting by Frank Dillon

PRINCELY PRETENSIONS

The opportunity for a second phase of improvements arose with Wellington's appointment as Prime Minister in 1828, when he had the use of 10 Downing Street (the Waterloo Banquet was held there in 1829). Wyatt wrote to Wellington on 3 May 1828 with estimates for a new wing to the west of Apsley House, in which to house the vast Waterloo Gallery, with a bedroom, dressing room and sitting room below. This was to cost £14,000, with a further £4,000 estimated for encasing the house in Bath stone and adding the portico over the new front door. The solid wall and gates in front of the house were replaced at this time with the high wrought-iron screen and gates to provide security (the turnpike was removed in 1825) and to accord with the new Hyde Park Screen which had been built between 1822 and 1825 by Decimus Burton (1800–1881).

Wellington took the opportunity to make several other alterations while these refurbishments were taking place. The main staircase was remodelled and its column screens removed. A similar screen was also taken out of the Piccadilly Drawing Room. Wyatt simplified much of the original Adam decoration, removing painted roundels from the ceilings and replacing pastel colours with cream and gilt. He also introduced vast plate-glass mirrors to make the most of the light that remained after he had lost windows on the west side to build the Waterloo Gallery. New furniture and furnishings were supplied by Thomas Dowbiggin & Co, with metalwork for the doors and the windows by J Bramah & Sons and plasterwork by Bernasconi and George Jackson & Sons.

The show-piece of these improvements was the Waterloo Gallery. This grand picture gallery had to be worthy of the masterpieces from the Spanish Royal Collection, by Correggio, Velázquez, Murillo, Rubens, Van Dyck and others, which King Ferdinand VII of Spain had allowed Wellington to keep. The gallery also had to impress visiting monarchs and function as the setting for the annual Waterloo Banquet. Since Benjamin Dean Wyatt's first series of alterations to Apsley House, his architectural style had moved on. Together with his brother, Matthew Cotes Wyatt (1777–1862), he had pioneered the introduction

Left: Detail of the Waterloo Gallery, the showpiece of the alterations to Apsley House carried out by Benjamin Dean Wyatt under Wellington

of the French revival style, known affectionately today as '*tous-les-Louis*' (from its use of design elements dating from the reigns of Louis XIV, XV and XVI). Belvoir Castle was remodelled on these lines by the two brothers in 1824, and Benjamin Dean Wyatt was commissioned the following year by the second son of King George III, the 'Grand Old' Duke of York, to create York House in London (subsequently renamed Lancaster House) to the same taste. Unfortunately the Duke of York died in 1827, hopelessly in debt to his builders, and although the new owner, the 2nd Marquis of Stafford, kept Wyatt on, he was no longer the chief architect. The Apsley House commission therefore came at a fortunate time for Wyatt, and he was able to continue where he had left off on his designs for a great gallery at York House.

REVIVAL STYLE

The new Waterloo Gallery revived the splendour of King Louis XIV's palace at Versailles. The *Galerie des Glaces* there provided the inspiration for Wyatt's mirrored walls but offered no design source for his ceiling, for at Versailles it is covered in paintings, as if floating above walls of light. The optimum display of the oil paintings in the Waterloo Gallery, however, required daylight to enter the room from above, through the ceiling. Wyatt chose to place a cupola at the centre of the gallery, which he may have derived from a

Above: The Waterloo Gallery showing the innovative ceiling designed to maximise light for viewing the masterpieces from the Spanish Royal Collection, many of which are still on display here today
Right: The Museum painted in 1853 by Thomas Shotter Boys (Victoria & Albert Museum)

design for the ceiling of 'le grand salon du Palais Royal' published in Paris between 1744 and 1748 by Gilles-Marie Oppenord. To either side of the cupola, Wyatt designed ceilings of intersecting circles; these follow an ancient pattern from a mausoleum that Wyatt found reproduced in a book by Robert Wood, *A General View of the Ruins of Palmyra* (London, 1756). The remainder of this expansive flat ceiling is made up of gilded plasterwork and glass panes, while the cove and cornice help to distribute the light into the room. Gilded putti flank six shields bearing the duke's coat of arms in the cove, and in each corner may be seen the badge and collar of the Order of the Garter. The walls were kept clear of decoration to afford maximum space for the duke's paintings, but the three royal portraits were given new carved picture frames in the French rococo-revival style, supplied by the duke's frame maker, Thomas Temple & Son, probably to Wyatt's design. They rose above three Siena marble chimneypieces originally designed by Wyatt for York House.

FINAL EXPENSES

By November 1828 architect and client had fallen out over costs and Wellington's friend, Mrs Arbuthnot, stepped in, noting 'when his house is the admiration of all London … I shall consider the merit all due to me'. The final cost of the extension and alterations was to be about £64,000. The yellow silk hangings were finally fitted in the gallery in March 1830. Still not satisfied, Wellington wrote to Wyatt on 24 October 1830 to complain that 'windows, doors, curtains, window shutters etc should be made so as to open and that with ease, to keep out the weather; and the chimnies not to smoke'. As Mrs Arbuthnot noted, 'he said the shame and ridicule of being so cheated and imposed upon, and the having been led on to an expenditure which must ruin his family, made him quite miserable'.

Wellington must have had enough of builders, for no further alterations were made to the house in his lifetime. The 2nd Duke introduced red damask in the gallery and the Minton mosaic floors and radiator covers in the entrance hall and inner hall, and moved the museum to its present location to display his father's valuable collection to best advantage. Thereafter the house was preserved with few alterations.

Memories of Apsley House

Victor Percival worked at Apsley House when management responsibility for public opening passed to the Victoria & Albert Museum in 1952.

'When I arrived at Apsley House, Park Lane wasn't here. It made a big difference to the setting, as you can imagine. I was responsible for most of the work involved in getting Apsley going as an efficient part of the Victoria & Albert Museum, and after that for its day-to-day administration. In 1966 I was promoted to Senior Research Assistant and Officer-in-Charge of Apsley House. I became a specialist on the Duke of Wellington, writing guidebooks to the house, giving radio talks and television interviews and supervising many banquets and events. I loved the job, mounting the exhibitions, putting the showcases in and travelling with loan collections to America, Germany and France.

'Apsley House was a shadow of its former self when the Victoria & Albert Museum took over. There were insufficient funds for the house to be kept up to standard. The Striped Drawing Room was all bare. It gave me the impression of being a workhouse – a very high-standard workhouse, I might say. The dining-room table was in the main state room [the Waterloo Gallery], with the chairs against the walls. When we came here the fabric was in strips on the walls. The Waterloo Gallery was used for various banquets and came to life on these occasions. My greatest regret is that the kitchens were not included in the gift. Some of the kitchen equipment went to the Museum of London and some to the kitchens at Brighton Pavilion.'

Right: Apsley House photographed in 1949, two years after it was established as the Wellington Museum by Act of Parliament

Above and right: The Portico Drawing Room (above) and the Waterloo Gallery (right) under wraps in 1943 during the Second World War

WELLINGTON'S SHRINE

Through the generosity of Gerald Wellesley, 7th Duke of Wellington, and through the passage of the Wellington Museum Act in 1947, part of the house was converted for public use as a museum and Apsley House opened to visitors in 1952, the centenary of the death of the 1st Duke of Wellington. A noted architect and Surveyor of the King's Works of Art, the 7th Duke was an expert on his great-grandfather, the 1st Duke. He also served as a member of the Advisory Council of the Victoria & Albert Museum, as Chairman of Trustees of the National Gallery and as a Trustee of the Wallace Collection.

Between 1961 and 1962 Park Lane was diverted to Hyde Park Corner, prompting the demolition of the houses immediately to the east and thereby cutting Apsley House off from Piccadilly. The forecourt coach house was demolished, the new east façade clad in Bath stone and the public underpasses were formed.

Much of the historic furniture belonging to Apsley House had not been accepted by the nation in 1947, to facilitate the use of some rooms as venues for government entertaining. A campaign to restore the interiors was launched in 1977 by the Department of Furniture and Woodwork at the Victoria & Albert Museum, and the resulting research, redecoration and redisplay of the collection between 1978 and 1982 set new standards for historic house interiors. Further restoration followed between 1992 and 1995. In 2004 responsibility for maintaining and opening Apsley House transferred to English Heritage.

As the restoration continues, Apsley House will regain the atmosphere of a London palace, as it was known by the monarchs, diplomats, soldiers and servants who visited, lived or worked there. Several works of art and furnishings not originally retained in the public rooms have been generously loaned for display by the Duke of Wellington's family, and can be appreciated in the original setting today. Eight fine rooms are now open to the public, while the 8th Duke of Wellington and his family still maintain their private apartments in the house. Meanwhile, the rich documentary and pictorial evidence that survives provides an exceptional record for this magnificent house.